THE
TELEVISION

Richard and Louise Spilsbury

KT-417-069

3 0116 01816114 9

www.raintreepublishers.co.uk
Visit our website to find out
more information about
Raintree books.

To order:
☎ Phone 0845 6044371
▤ Fax +44 (0) 1865 312263
▣ Email myorders@raintreepublishers.co.uk

Customers from outside the UK please telephone +44 1865 312262

Raintree is an imprint of Capstone Global Library
Limited, a company incorporated in England and Wales
having its registered office at 7 Pilgrim Street, London,
EC4V 6LB – Registered company number: 6695582

Text © Capstone Global Library Limited 2012
First published in hardback in 2012
First published in paperback in 2013
The moral rights of the proprietor have been asserted.

All rights reserved. No part of this publication may be
reproduced in any form or by any means (including
photocopying or storing it in any medium by electronic
means and whether or not transiently or incidentally to
some other use of this publication) without the written
permission of the copyright owner, except in accordance
with the provisions of the Copyright, Designs and
Patents Act 1988 or under the terms of a licence issued
by the Copyright Licensing Agency, Saffron House,
6–10 Kirby Street, London EC1N 8TS (www.cla.co.uk).
Applications for the copyright owner's written
permission should be addressed to the publisher.

Edited by Louise Galpine and Laura Knowles
Designed by Philippa Jenkins
Illustrations by KJA-artists.com
Original illustrations © Capstone Global Library
    Limited 2012
Illustrated by KJA-artists.com
Picture research by Mica Brancic
Originated by Capstone Global Library Limited
Printed and bound in China by CTPS

ISBN 978 1 406 22272 2 (hardback)
15 14 13 12 11
10 9 8 7 6 5 4 3 2 1

ISBN 978 1 406 22279 1 (paperback)
16 15 14 13 12
10 9 8 7 6 5 4 3 2 1

British Library Cataloguing in Publication Data
Spilsbury, Louise.
The television. -- (Tales of invention)
621.3'88'009-dc22
A full catalogue record for this book is available from
the British Library.

Acknowledgements
We would like to thank the following for permission to
reproduce photographs: **Acknowledgements**
We would like to thank the following for permission
to reproduce photographs: Alamy pp. **20** (© Interfoto),
27 (© Artur Marciniec); Corbis pp. **4** (Reuters/© Peter
Macdiarmid), **10** (© Bettmann), **12** (© Bettmann),
14 (© Bettmann), **15** (© Bettmann), **16** (© Bettmann),
17 (© Bettmann), **18** (© Bettmann), **22** (Reuters/
© Hannibal Hanschke), **26** (Blend Images/© Colin
Anderson); Getty Images pp. **11** (Hulton Archive/
Keystone), **21** (CBS Photo Archive), **24** (Photodisc/
Ed Freeman), **25** (Stone/Flying Colours); Library of
Congress pp. **8**, **13**; Science Photo Library pp. **5**
(Adam Hart-Davis), **9** (RIA Novosti), **7**.

Cover photograph of a woman demonstrating a
television set at a radio exhibition in 1938 reproduced
with permission of Corbis/© Hulton-Deutsch Collection.

We would like to thank Walter Podrazik for his
invaluable help in the preparation of this book.

Every effort has been made to contact copyright holders
of material reproduced in this book. Any omissions will
be rectified in subsequent printings if notice is given to
the publisher.

Disclaimer
All the internet addresses (URLs) given in this book
were valid at the time of going to press. However, due
to the dynamic nature of the internet, some addresses
may have changed, or sites may have changed or
ceased to exist since publication. While the author
and publisher regret any inconvenience this may cause
readers, no responsibility for any such changes can be
accepted by either the author or the publisher.

CONTENTS

Look for these boxes

Biographies

These boxes tell you about the life of inventors, the dates when they lived, and their important discoveries.

Setbacks

Here we tell you about the experiments that didn't work, the failures, and the accidents.

EUREKA!

These boxes tell you about important events and discoveries, and what inspired them.

Any words appearing in the text in bold, **like this**, are explained in the glossary.

TIMELINE

2011 – The timeline shows you when important discoveries and inventions were made.

Most of us take television for granted. We can switch it on at any time to see news, films, sports, nature programmes, and so on. But what is television? It is a way of sending and receiving images (pictures) and sounds through wires, air, or space as waves of energy. Television cameras convert action into **signals**, or patterns of **electricity**. The television sets we have in our homes are **receivers**. The receivers convert the electricity back into programmes we can see and hear.

Huge, modern TV screens allow large crowds to watch events on television.

1834 – William George Horner invents the zoetrope

1837 – Samuel Morse demonstrates an electric **telegraph**

1830

1835

Moving pictures at home

Before television was invented, the only moving pictures most people saw were at the cinema. Only a few people saw moving images at home, for example using toys such as a zoetrope The.zoetrope is a hollow drum with slits around the edge and a sequence of different images inside. The images look as if they are moving when the viewer spins the drum and looks through the slits from the outside.

What people saw with zoetropes was quite different to what we watch on television today. The development and spread of television took many decades and involved many inventors.

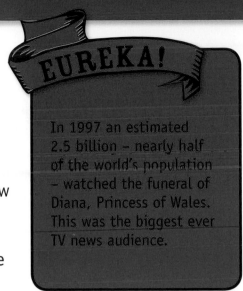

In 1997 an estimated 2.5 billion – nearly half of the world's population – watched the funeral of Diana, Princess of Wales. This was the biggest ever TV news audience.

The zoetrope tricks the brain into seeing differences between images as movements of the same image.

In the mid- to late-1800s, people communicated by **telegraph**, which sent words using different **signals** through wires. In 1883, Paul Nipkow invented a way to send images in a similar way, using metal discs with holes in. Up close, an image, such as a drawing, is made of a pattern of light and dark. **Scanning** converts that pattern, line by line, into a sequence of signals. One **Nipkow disc** scanned an image and a second disc used the signals to recreate the image.

How a Nipkow disc works

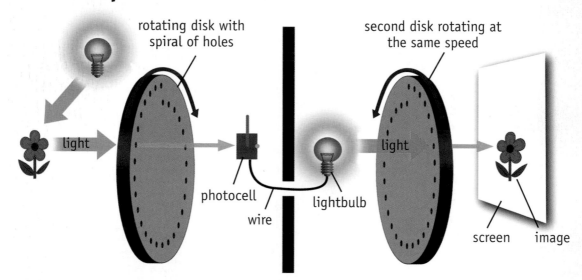

rotating disk with spiral of holes

second disk rotating at the same speed

light

photocell

wire

lightbulb

light

screen   image

1. The disc has a spiral pattern of holes. When the disc **rotates**, each hole moves across the image.

2. The amount of light from the image passing through each hole is detected by a **photocell**. This is a special bulb covered with a substance called selenium, which conducts more **electricity** when it is lit up than when dark.

3. The photocell's electrical signal passes through a wire to a bulb, making the bulb glow or remain dark.

4. Light from the bulb shines through a second rotating disc, and shows the image on a screen.

Paul Nipkow *(1860–1940)*

German inventor Paul Nipkow was a student when he designed his scanner. Although the invention successfully sent an image from London to Paris, few people could see a practical use for it. Nipkow spent most of his life as a railway engineer.

Seeing the invisible

Scientists studying atoms, the tiny building blocks of all matter, realized that they contained **electrons**. But electrons are a bit like moving pieces of electricity that are impossible to see! In 1897, German scientist Ferdinand Braun invented a device called the **cathode ray tube** that could show where electrons were.

The cathode ray tube is a glass tube with no air inside that contains a part called a cathode. When electricity moves through the cathode, it heats up and sends out a beam of electrons through the tube. A spot of light appears at the flat end of the tube. This happens because the glass at that end is painted with a chemical that glows when electrons hit it.

Ferdinand Braun shared the 1909 Nobel Prize for Physics with Guglielmo Marconi, who invented the radio.

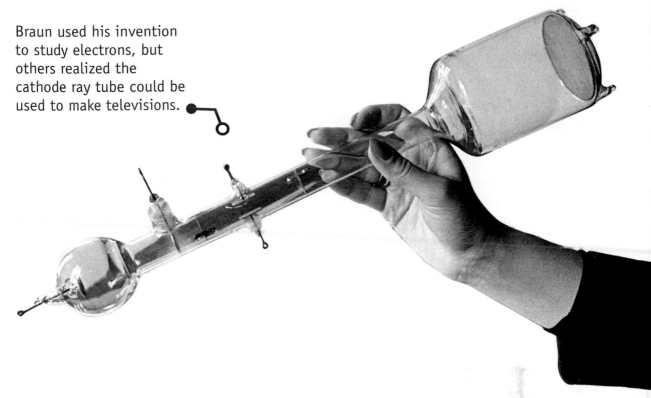

Braun used his invention to study electrons, but others realized the cathode ray tube could be used to make televisions.

The next step

Braun then started to experiment with his invention. He discovered that **magnets** could pull or push the electron beam just as they would an iron bar. Using magnets he could make the spot of light move to different parts of the screen. Braun also varied the amount of electricity going in to the electrode. This changed the size of the electron beam and therefore the brightness of the light on the screen.

Setbacks

In 1908 British engineer Alan Campbell-Swinton gave a lecture. In it, he said that a cathode ray tube could show complete images made of dots of light sent through wires. However, he never managed to come up with a working model.

9

1873 – Willoughby Smith and Joseph May accidentally discover that more electricity flows through selenium in light than it does in the dark

1870   1875

In 1922 Charles Jenkins invented a way of sending images without wires. His system **scanned** images in a similar way to **Nipkow discs**. **Signals** from the scan made **electrons** vibrate in a machine called a **transmitter**.

The electrons produced **radio waves**, which are fast-moving vibrations of energy. Aerials on **receivers** could capture some of the waves. The receiver converted the radio waves back into signals, and then into tiny images on a screen. People viewed these through a built-in magnifying glass. Jenkins made a famous demonstration of his system in 1923 when he sent an image of US President Warren G. Harding 210 kilometres (130 miles) across the United States, from Washington to Philadelphia.

Here, Charles Jenkins is showing his equipment, which he claimed could transmit moving images through radio waves.

10

Baird's breakthrough

On 25 March 1925, Scottish inventor John Logie Baird demonstrated a **mechanical** TV in a large store in London. It showed moving images of drawings scanned with Nipkow discs and transmitted by radio. A few months later, Baird transmitted images of a talking puppet called Stooky Bill from his tiny laboratory. He used a puppet because the lamps used to light up the televised subject so it could be scanned were too hot for actors. Even so, Stooky Bill's hair was burnt and his lips cracked from the heat!

This is the equipment used to create the tiny, blurred television image of Stooky Bill.

Setbacks

Charles Jenkins claimed to have sent Radio-Movies (moving images as radio waves) in 1923, but there are no proper records. His first transmission was in June 1925, just three months after Baird!

1883 – Paul Nipkow invents the Nipkow disc to scan images (see page 6)

1885   1890

John Logie Baird showed how his invention worked by transmitting his own image.

Improvements

After the first television, Baird improved his invention. He used bigger discs with more holes. These scanned images with higher **resolution** as there were more lines making up the image. The discs **rotated** faster so images replaced each other more quickly and flickered less on screen. He used **photocells** that needed less light to make a signal, so television could be filmed using weaker, cooler lamps, or even daylight. Baird also added a device called an **amplifier** which made the signal stronger. This meant it could be transmitted further using radio waves. By 1928, Baird had sent a television signal from London to New York.

1897 – J. J. Thomson discovers electrons. Ferdinand Braun invents the **cathode ray tube** (see page 8).

John Logie Baird *(1888–1946)*

In his twenties, John Logie Baird tried to make artificial (fake) diamonds and succeeded in inventing socks that helped prevent foot infections. He made his first TV out of materials he found in his laboratory, such as old biscuit tins and bike lamps!

Electronic television

In 1927, American Philo Farnsworth invented the first completely **electronic** television. Electronic machines work by controlling the flow of electrons rather than mechanical parts. Farnsworth's TV camera was a **cathode ray tube** with a special screen inside that produced electrons wherever light fell. **Magnets** bent the electrons line by line into a tube that converted them into signals. In the receiver's cathode ray tube, the signals were pieced back into images with 300 lines of resolution. That was 10 times more than Baird's first **broadcasts**.

EUREKA!

Farnsworth was driving a tractor when he invented his TV. He realized that a moving electron beam could scan an image line by line in a similar way to how he ploughed his family's fields.

Philo Farnsworth's electronic television produced a much clearer image than earlier inventions.

Philo Taylor Farnsworth *(1906–1971)*

Philo Farnsworth decided to invent electrical machines when he was young, living on a farm in Idaho, USA. In 1922, aged 14, he decided that Nipkow discs would not move fast enough to scan images and that moving electrons were the answer. After going to college to learn more, Farnsworth finally built his TV in 1927, with the help of money given by some local businessmen. By then Philo had married his college sweetheart Pem who helped him with his invention. She was also the first ever person broadcast on electronic TV!

1920 – Charles Jenkins sends still images using radio waves (see page 10)

1915   1920

In the late 1920s, **mechanical** televisions were demonstrated to the public by Baird in the United Kingdom and by Charles Jenkins in the United States. The British Broadcasting Corporation (BBC) started **transmitting** television programmes to the UK public using Baird's system in the 1930s. By the early 1930s, thousands of people were watching these programmes on television **receivers**. These receivers were mostly supplied as kits that people had to put together themselves.

Early programmes were experiments to see what was possible with the new invention. For example, the BBC **broadcast** a strange play with three actors called *The Man with the Flower in his Mouth*. One of the first stars of US television was a small statue of the cartoon character Felix the Cat **rotating** on a turntable!

Mechanical TV cameras of the 1930s were big, but some could produce very clear images.

1923 – Vladimir Zworykin invents the iconoscope

1925 – John Logie Baird demonstrates the first working TV to the public. Charles Jenkins transmits his first Radio-Movies (see page 11).

1927 – Philo Farnsworth invents the first electronic TV (see page 14)

1920　　　　　　　　　　　　　　　　　1925

The American public was amazed at the clear images when RCA demonstrated their new electronic TV cameras at the World's Fair in 1939.

Electronic television takes over

During the 1930s, various inventors made **electronic** TV cameras based on Farnsworth's ideas. In 1937 the BBC started to use Isaac Shoenberg's version instead of Baird's mechanical camera, as it was less bulky and produced better images. In the United States, Vladimir Zworykin developed a new, sensitive camera for US television company RCA. This was called the iconoscope and it became widely used there.

Setbacks

In 1935, Farnsworth won a court case against RCA which proved Zworykin had used his electronic television idea. RCA was ordered to pay Farnsworth money for his invention. However, as a well-established business, RCA delayed payments and was then able to make money from their electronic TVs once Farnsworth's **patent** ran out in 1947.

1928 – Baird's mechanical TV sends moving images by **radio waves** across the Atlantic Ocean (see page 12). Baird demonstrates mechanical **3D** TV (see page 26). The first US TV station is started by Charles Jenkins.

1930   1935

Popular machine

During World War II (1939–1945), many electronics factories were busy making things for the war, not televisions. However, by the 1950s factories were producing the receivers people wanted to buy, as a wider range of programmes was **broadcast**. This included the first soap operas on US television, such as *Guiding Light*, which ran from 1952 to 2009. Soap operas are ongoing serialized stories stretched out over years in regular episodes. They got their name because they were first sponsored on radio by soap companies!

Watching television became very popular. For example, over 50 per cent of the UK population watched the 1953 coronation of Queen Elizabeth II on TV compared to 30 per cent listening on radio. As not everyone had their own receivers, many viewers went to neighbours' houses to watch.

I Love Lucy was the most popular US TV series of the early 1950s. In this episode, the characters argued about breaking their TV receiver!

Colour television

Colour televisions were first invented in the late 1930s by Peter Goldmark, but most people still watched black-and-white TVs during the 1940s and 50s. This was because colour TVs were very expensive, showed unrealistic colours, and did not work well. By the 1960s, more people were buying improved colour TVs. Colour **cathode ray tubes** fired three separate **electron** beams through a thin metal grid with thousands of tiny holes called a shadow mask. The mask directed the electrons against three sorts of dots on the screen that glowed red, blue, or green. The combination of these coloured dots, or **pixels**, formed images.

Setbacks

Parts in some early colour receivers got very hot. Viewers were told to stay near their TV for an hour after they switched it off in case their homes caught fire!

This diagram shows how cathode ray colour televisions work.

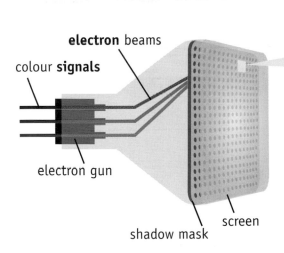

electron beams
colour **signals**
electron gun
shadow mask
screen

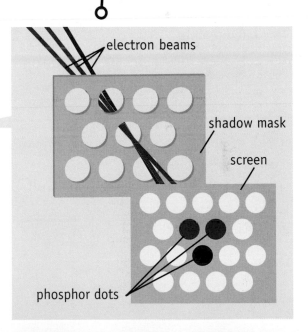

electron beams
shadow mask
screen
phosphor dots

1944 – John Logie Baird invents a completely electronic colour TV

1947 – Alfred Schroeder invents the shadow mask for colour TV

1948 – Margaret and John Walson create the first **cable TV** network (see page 20)

1945

1950

Better reception

John and Margaret Walson owned a TV shop in a hilly town in the United States, but sold few receivers because the picture was fuzzy. The hills blocked radio **signals** from reaching their receivers. In 1948 the Walsons fixed an aerial at the top of a nearby mountain, where there was clear TV reception, and laid a cable from this to their shop. Locals paid for the Walsons to link their homes to the cable to get a clear picture. This was the first **cable TV**. Today's cable TV companies offer hundreds of channels for customers.

Setbacks

The first TV controls were wired to the television. Later, remote (wireless) controls operated the TV using a flash of light. But other household lights and bright sunlight could accidentally change channels!

This large remote control was used in the 1950s.

1955 – Zenith makes the first remote control

Using satellites

There is a limit to how far TV programmes can be broadcast by **radio waves**. Radio waves travel in straight lines – they cannot travel around the Earth because it has a curved shape. To send programmes worldwide, TV companies beam their programmes straight up to TV **satellites**. The satellites then bounce radio signals back to Earth. People with satellite dishes can receive the signals. The first TV satellite, the *Telstar*, was carried to space on a rocket in 1962, but today there are hundreds of them.

Satellite TV made it possible for people to watch live TV from the surface of the moon in 1969.

21

1962 – The *Telstar* satellite is sent into space

1964 – Donald Bitzer and Gene Slottow invent the earliest **plasma screen** in the United States (see page 23)

1960

1965

Baird's first TV showed images 6 centimetres (2.5 inches) high. Ever since then, **receivers** have generally been getting bigger to show bigger images. Big **cathode ray tube** receivers are bulky, heavy, and use up a lot of **electricity**. Today, all new TV receivers have flat screens. They are light, thin, and energy efficient for their size. Look closely at the surface of a flat screen TV and you can see it is divided up into millions of **pixels**. Each pixel is made of red, blue, and green **subpixels**. Images are made on-screen when the subpixels flick on or off.

Flat screen TVs can be made much bigger than older cathode-ray tube televisions because they do not need heavy, fragile glass tubes inside.

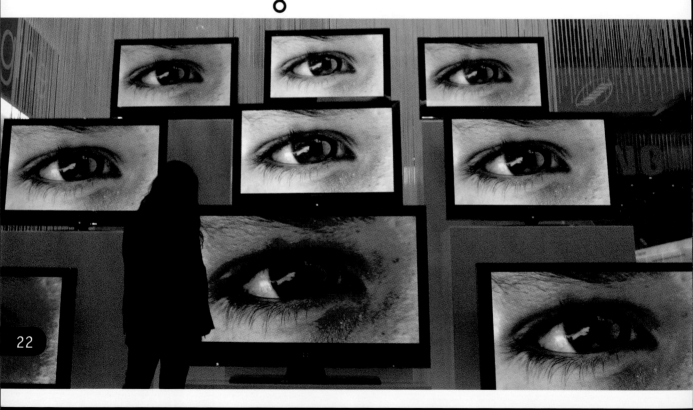

22

Two types

There are two main types of flat screens. **Plasma screens** were invented in 1964 by Donald Bitzer and Gene Slottow. The screens use tiny bulbs filled with very hot, glowing gas to light up subpixels. **LCD screens**, which were invented in 1967 by James Fergason, work differently. In LCD screens, the subpixels are rather like tiny, coloured sunglasses in front of a lit-up screen. The amount of light they let through to form an image on screen depends on a special liquid. This can become more or less **transparent** depending on the size of the **electronic signal**.

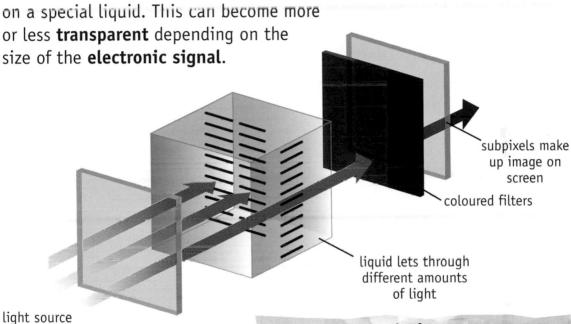

subpixels make up image on screen

coloured filters

liquid lets through different amounts of light

light source

These are the four main layers of an LCD screen. Electronic signals control how much light is let through the liquid layer.

Setbacks

In early plasma screens, subpixels sometimes stayed permanently black, usually in the shape of a word or other shape that had remained on screen for a long time!

23

Carrying more information

There are many sizes of **radio waves** and only some are used to carry television signals. Others are reserved for other purposes, such as for airline pilots to communicate. In the 1990s, countries worldwide realized there would soon be too many channels to fit on to the TV radio waves. They worked together to develop **digital TV**.

With digital TV, programmes are converted into computer code that takes up less space than older signals on radio waves. This means the waves can carry more channels. Receivers piece the code back together into programmes. Viewers can also interact with digital TV, for example by pressing the red button to take part in TV quizzes. By 2010, around 13 countries had switched to **broadcasting** just digital signals.

The Pearl Oriental tower in Shanghai, China, broadcasts digital TV programmes.

Home cinema

Watching television today can feel like being in a small cinema! Many flat screens can display more pixels per square inch to show **high-definition** (HD) images. Some have **surround sound**, invented by Peter Scheiber in 1967. Television signals contain separate image and sound parts. Surround sound is a way of dividing up the sound part into different pieces. Each piece makes a separate loudspeaker work. When the loudspeakers are placed around a room, the viewer hears the sounds as if they are happening around them.

 With better screens, digital signals, and surround sound, people today can enjoy a much richer TV experience than in the past.

Setbacks

Scheiber invited Ray Dolby to his home to show how his surround sound invention worked. Dolby quickly made and marketed something similar. The Dolby company became rich by selling surround sound systems!

25

The newest types of **receivers** on sale are **three-dimensional (3D)** TVs. The first one was introduced in 2010 by Samsung. Programmes or films for 3D TV normally look blurred because they contain two very slightly different images that almost overlap. If viewers wear special **electronic** glasses, the images overlap into a clear picture. Some 3D screens have special textured screens sending different images to each eye so viewers do not need glasses. Inventors are already working on special TV screens that will project coloured light from different angles. This creates moving images that can be viewed from different sides.

In future, what we see coming out of 3D TV screens might be even more realistic than today.

EUREKA!

In 1928 John Logie Baird demonstrated the first 3D TV. He did this by showing slightly different images alternately for the left eye, then right eye so fast that the viewer saw a 3D image.

26

1998 – The United Kingdom and United States start the **digital TV** switchover

1995

2000

 Will channel hopping look like this in the future?

Internet TV

The invention of television has allowed global audiences to experience entertainment, news, and sights from around the world. There are now around 1.5 billion TV receivers on the planet. That is about one for every four people! Television audiences are growing for live events, such as the Olympics. However, many people are now watching recordings of programmes on the Internet using computers and mobile phones. Some TV channels have started creating programmes just for the Internet. The first Internet TV **broadcasts** were made in the late 1990s. In future people will be able to surf through thousands of channels and films on TV receivers at home.

2006 – Luxembourg is the first country to broadcast just digital TV

2009 – US officially completes the transition to digital

2010 – Samsung produces the first electronic 3D **high-definition TV**

2005

2010

TIMELINE

1834
William George Horner invents the zoetrope

1837
Samuel Morse demonstrates an electric **telegraph**

1873
Willoughby Smith and Joseph May accidentally discover that more **electricity** flows through selenium in light than it does in the dark

1938
RCA makes the first US television sets

1937
BBC **broadcasts** using only electronic television

1928
Baird's **mechanical** television sends moving images by radio waves across the Atlantic Ocean. Baird demonstrates mechanical **3D** TV.
The first US TV station is started by Charles Jenkins.

1939
Peter Goldmark invents a colour TV that uses spinning discs

1944
John Logie Baird invents a completely electronic colour TV

1947
Alfred Schroeder invents the shadow mask for colour TV

2010
Samsung produce the first electronic 3D **high-definition TV**

1998
The United Kingdom and United States start the **digital TV** switchover

1970
Fergason and his team produce the first **LCD** TV

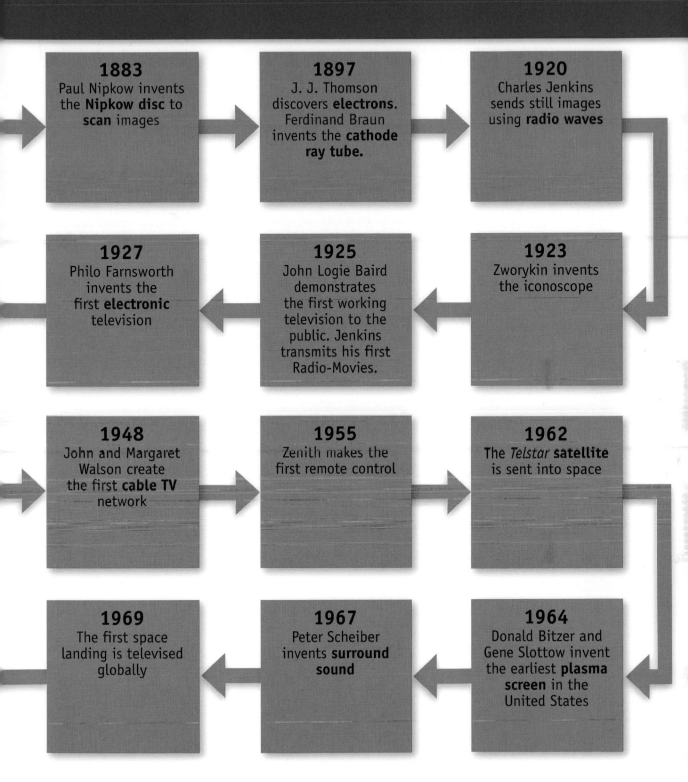

1883
Paul Nipkow invents the **Nipkow disc** to **scan** images

1897
J. J. Thomson discovers **electrons**. Ferdinand Braun invents the **cathode ray tube.**

1920
Charles Jenkins sends still images using **radio waves**

1927
Philo Farnsworth invents the first **electronic** television

1925
John Logie Baird demonstrates the first working television to the public. Jenkins transmits his first Radio-Movies.

1923
Zworykin invents the iconoscope

1948
John and Margaret Walson create the first **cable TV** network

1955
Zenith makes the first remote control

1962
The *Telstar* **satellite** is sent into space

1969
The first space landing is televised globally

1967
Peter Scheiber invents **surround sound**

1964
Donald Bitzer and Gene Slottow invent the earliest **plasma screen** in the United States

GLOSSARY

amplifier device used to increase the strength of a signal

broadcast send out a programme that can be viewed on TV receivers

cable TV television system where signals move through wires to viewers and not via radio waves

cathode ray tube device in which images are made when electrons hit a glass screen

digital TV television system where sound and image signals are sent as computer (digital) code

electricity form of energy from the flow of an electric charge

electron tiny particle with a negative charge usually found in an atom

electronic something that works using the flow of electrons

high-definition TV television system that shows much more detailed images than normal TV

LCD screen stands for Liquid Crystal Display. This is a flat electronic display panel that filters light to produce an image.

magnet device or object that attracts some metals, such as iron or steel

mechanical describes a machine that works mainly using moving parts, for example an engine turns wheels in a car

Nipkow disc disc with holes for converting light and dark patterns into signals, and signals into light patterns

patent official proof that an invention, idea, or process was the idea of a particular person, and protection from it being copied

photocell device creating a signal size depending on the amount of light it is exposed to

pixel smallest point or dot making up an image

plasma screen thin, flat electronic display panel using glowing gas bulbs to produce an image

radio wave type of radiation that moves fast and straight like light

receiver device that receives a signal and converts it into sound and images

resolution measure of the detail with which an image appears on a screen, usually shown in pixels or dots per inch

rotate turn around or spin

satellite object put into space to move around Earth, often to transmit radio and other signals

scan change images into patterns of electricity or signals

signal message, usually sent as sound, light, or radio wave

subpixel building block of a pixel

surround sound system in cinemas or for televisions that reproduces sound from loudspeakers all around the audience

telegraph system for sending messages by radio waves or electric wires

three-dimensional (3D) having, or seeming to have, height, width, and depth. Real objects are 3D, but pictures on paper are not.

transmitter device that sends out a signal as a radio wave

transparent see-through

Books

The Boy who Invented TV: The Story of Philo Farnsworth, Kathleen Krull (Alfred A. Knopf, 2009)

Inventing the Television (Breakthrough Inventions), Joanne Richter (Crabtree, 2006)

Inventor's Secret Scrapbook (White Wolves), Chris Oxlade (A&C Black, 2011)

Television (Behind the Scenes), Sarah Medina (Wayland, 2009)

Websites

www.mztv.com
Enter the virtual museum to learn more about the pioneers of television, what people said about TV, and many other interesting exhibits.

www.makingthemodernworld.org.uk
Type "television" into the search engine on this website to see pictures and facts about TV inventions and inventors.

www.bbc.co.uk/history/historic_figures/baird_logie.shtml
Visit this website to learn more detail about the life of John Logie Baird.

www.museum.tv
Find out more about television through The Museum of Broadcast Communications in Chicago's website.

Places to visit

National Media Museum
Bradford, West Yorkshire BD1 1NQ
www.nationalmediamuseum.org.uk

Science Museum
South Kensington, London SW7 2DD
www.sciencemuseum.org.uk

INDEX

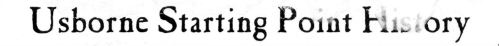

Who built the pyramids?

Jane Chisholm & Struan Reid

Illustrated by Sue Stitt
Designed by Vicki Groombridge & Diane Thistlethwaite

History consultant: Dr. Anne Millard

CONTENTS

Usborne Quicklinks

For links to websites where you can find out lots more about
Ancient Egypt and the Egyptians, go to the Usborne Quicklinks website at
www.usborne.com/quicklinks and type in the keywords **starting pyramids**.
Please follow the internet safety guidelines displayed at the Usborne Quicklinks website.

3 0116 02002446 7

Who built the pyramids?

Tens of thousands of ordinary Egyptian men, led by architects, engineers and other experts. Most of the builders worked for the king for a few months every year as a sort of tax.

Step pyramid

How old are the pyramids?

Incredibly old. The first were built nearly 5,000 years ago. Some are in ruins, but many are in amazingly good condition to this day.

Desert police, called Medjay, patrol the western frontier with big dogs.

Where are they?

In Egypt, on the west bank of the Nile, Egypt's great river.

A few people live in the desert oases – small green areas, with water and a few palm trees. They trade salt, cattle and crafts.

This is the Valley of the Kings. It's where the later kings are buried, after people stopped building pyramids. You can find out more on pages 8-9.

Mediterranean Sea

The Nile Delta. It's very green and marshy here.

Forts on Egypt's frontiers keep out invaders.

Great Pyramid and Sphinx

Stone for the pyramids is quarried here.

Red Sea

Memphis, the capital of Egypt in the Old Kingdom

Trading ships set out from here for Punt in East Africa.

Nearly everyone lives and farms along the Nile.

Everybody travels by boat in Egypt. You can see a lot of Egyptian boats on pages 20-21.

Away from the Nile, everywhere else is desert. Egyptians call it the Red Land.

Thebes, the great religious city of Egypt in the New Kingdom

Just south of Egypt are Nubia and Kush. For a long time, they were ruled by Egypt.

The Nile is a very long river. It begins in the mountains and lakes of East Africa.

Gold is mined here.

2

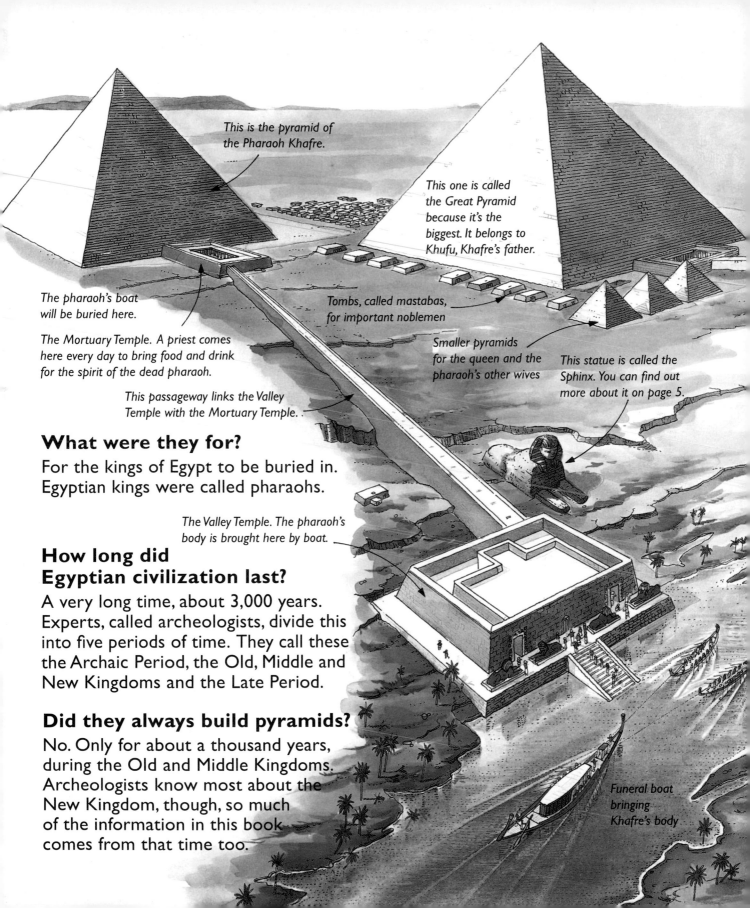

This is the pyramid of the Pharaoh Khafre.

This one is called the Great Pyramid because it's the biggest. It belongs to Khufu, Khafre's father.

The pharaoh's boat will be buried here.

Tombs, called mastabas, for important noblemen

The Mortuary Temple. A priest comes here every day to bring food and drink for the spirit of the dead pharaoh.

Smaller pyramids for the queen and the pharaoh's other wives

This statue is called the Sphinx. You can find out more about it on page 5.

This passageway links the Valley Temple with the Mortuary Temple.

What were they for?

For the kings of Egypt to be buried in. Egyptian kings were called pharaohs.

The Valley Temple. The pharaoh's body is brought here by boat.

How long did Egyptian civilization last?

A very long time, about 3,000 years. Experts, called archeologists, divide this into five periods of time. They call these the Archaic Period, the Old, Middle and New Kingdoms and the Late Period.

Did they always build pyramids?

No. Only for about a thousand years, during the Old and Middle Kingdoms. Archeologists know most about the New Kingdom, though, so much of the information in this book comes from that time too.

Funeral boat bringing Khafre's body

Why are pyramids pyramid-shaped?

Good question. No one is absolutely sure. The very first pyramids had steps up the sides. Experts believe this was meant to be a giant staircase to help the dead pharaoh climb to heaven.

Later pyramids had smooth sides – perhaps to look like the rays of the sun. The Egyptian sun god Re was one of their most important gods.

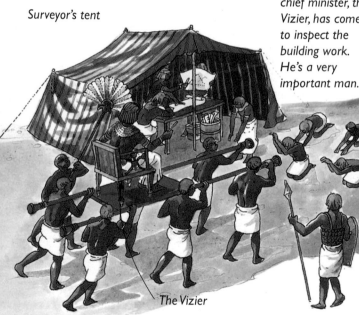

The blocks of stone are dragged up the ramp.

Men pour water onto the ramp and put logs under the sledges. All this helps them move more smoothly.

The pharaoh's chief minister, the Vizier, has come to inspect the building work. He's a very important man.

Surveyor's tent

The workers are hoping he'll be pleased with progress.

The Vizier

Can you spot the irritating fly?

Carpenters

How big are they?

That depends. Some are not very big, but others are enormous. At 146m (480ft) high, the Great Pyramid is as tall as some skyscrapers. It contains over two million blocks of stone. Some of the largest weigh over two tons or tonnes.

Aren't they a little big for tombs?

The Egyptians didn't think so. They thought their pharaohs were so special that they had to have the biggest and best of everything. Also, the higher the pyramid, the closer they <u>would be</u> to heaven.

How were they built?

By dragging the huge blocks of stone up huge earth ramps. Experts disagree about exactly how these were arranged. But the ramps were probably raised and lengthened every time a new layer of stones was added.

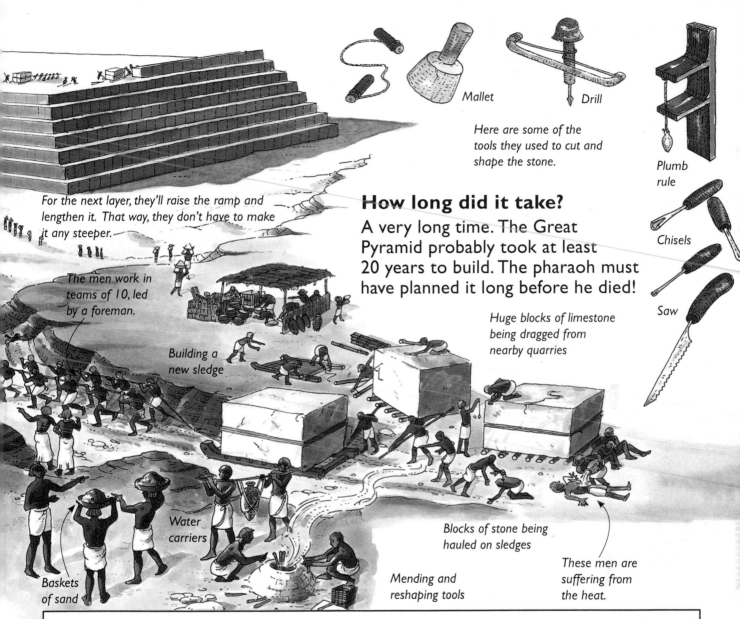

Mallet

Drill

Here are some of the tools they used to cut and shape the stone.

Plumb rule

Chisels

Saw

For the next layer, they'll raise the ramp and lengthen it. That way, they don't have to make it any steeper.

The men work in teams of 10, led by a foreman.

Building a new sledge

How long did it take?

A very long time. The Great Pyramid probably took at least 20 years to build. The pharaoh must have planned it long before he died!

Huge blocks of limestone being dragged from nearby quarries

Water carriers

Baskets of sand

Mending and reshaping tools

Blocks of stone being hauled on sledges

These men are suffering from the heat.

Were the workers badly treated?

Not at all. Archeologists have discovered the barracks where the workers lived, and the kitchens that made their food, which was excellent. They even had doctors ready to treat sick or injured men.

Did you know?

Near one of the pyramids is an enormous statue with the head of a pharaoh and a lion's body. It is called the Sphinx, and shows a version of the Sun God, Re, guarding the site.

5

What was inside a pyramid?

Not much (considering how big pyramids are). The insides were mostly solid stone, with long narrow passages. The pharaohs were buried with all kinds of amazing treasures, but they were all stolen long ago.

What is a mummy?

A body that is embalmed or preserved, so it doesn't decay, even over thousands of years. The Egyptians believed that doing this would mean that the person could carry on living in the Next World.

How did they preserve the bodies?

By finding ways of drying them out. Follow the pictures to see how they did this.

These pictures show how a mummy was made in the New Kingdom. In the background, you can see an outline of the Great Pyramid sliced in half.

1. First, they take out the internal organs, such as the heart and lungs, and put them in jars called canopic jars.

Canopic jars

Natron

2. Then they cover the body all over with a salt called natron, to dry it out. After several days, the insides are stuffed with linen, sawdust, natron, sweet-smelling herbs and spices.

Burial chanber

Passageways

3. Next, the body is wrapped tightly with bandages, with lucky charms called amulets between the layers. They use huge amounts of bandages. Then a mask is placed over the face.

Anubis mask

4. Finally, a priest comes to say prayers. He wears a mask on his head to look like the jackal god Anubis, god of embalming.

Mummies in the New Kingdom were put in a nest of two or three human-shaped coffins, like these. These were put inside a huge stone coffin, called a sarcophagus.

The coffins were painted with pictures of gods and godddesses and picture writing (called hieroglyphics).

Outer coffin

Inner coffin

Mask fits over face

Bandaged body

This is a wooden coffin from the Middle Kingdom. It's even more richly decorated inside.

The coffins buried in pyramids would have been simple box-shaped ones, like this one.

Why is it called a mummy?

The name comes from mumiyah, the Arabic word for bitumen, a sort of tar used on modern roads. When archeologists first found the bodies, they thought they must have been dipped in tar because they were so dark.

Didn't the mummies smell bad?

Not if the embalmers worked quickly before the body had a chance to decay. After it had been dried out and properly stuffed, it would have smelled lovely!

Were ordinary people mummified?

No. Only the very rich could afford the full treatment, although there were cheaper versions. But archeologists have found literally millions of animal mummies. These represented particular gods or goddesses. They include cats, dogs, birds, baboons and crocodiles.

Mummified cat

7

Why did they stop building pyramids?

Nobody knows for sure. It might have been because pyramids were so enormous that they attracted all the robbers for miles around. They were also very expensive to build and needed a huge number of workers.

Were all the pyramids robbed?

They were completely cleaned out! Within a thousand years, every single mummy and piece of treasure had been stolen. Pyramid designers tried all kinds of tricks to stop the robbers, but they still managed to get in.

Where did they bury their pharaohs after that?

In tombs cut deep inside rocky cliffs in a hidden-away valled called the Valley of the Kings. But, even though these tombs were difficult to get at and heavily guarded, in the end most of these were robbed too. Can you spot three robbers lying in wait?

This is a funeral procession to the Valley of the Kings.

This chest contains the canopic jars. You can find out what they are on page 6.

These soldiers are meant to be on guard, but they are having an argument instead.

The Chief Priest rides on the funeral boat. He's burning incense. It smells nice and is supposed to carry prayers up to heaven in the smoke.

Pharaoh's coffin

These women are priestesses. They cry at all the funerals.

The Queen and her two children. The boy is the new pharaoh.

What were the tombs like inside?

The best ones were absolutely amazing. Rooms crammed with treasures made of gold and precious stones, clothes, furniture, pots, pans, statues, paintings, writings and even chariots. The walls and ceilings were brightly painted all over.

Pharaoh's chariot

This man is upset because he has dropped a valuable box.

Food, furniture, jewels and treasures for the tomb.

This snake is making the horses nervous.

How do we know so much about the Egyptians?

Because of all the things they left in their tombs. The hot, dry climate meant that everything dried out, instead of rotting away.

These are just some of the things the archeologists found inside the tomb of the young pharaoh Tutankhamun.

Is there really a mummy's curse?

No, of course not. It's just some silly gossip that spread after Tutankhamun's tomb was discovered, over 70 years ago. Lord Carnarvon, one of the leaders of the expedition, was bitten by a mosquito, got blood poisoning, and died suddenly. A few people who liked a good story began to suggest that the pharaoh was angry at having his tomb disturbed and had put a curse on the archeologists.

Who ruled Egypt?

The kings, or pharaohs. They were so important that the Egyptians even believed they were gods. Each pharaoh was supposed to be descended from the sun god, called Re, who was the very first King of Egypt.

Were the pharaohs rich?

Enormously. Egypt was a very rich country and the pharaoh owned absolutely everything in it. He had not just one, but several palaces, and he moved from one to another.

Pharaoh

Queen

A scribe (you can find out what he does on page 30)

This courtier's fan is made of the very best ostrich feathers.

Guards

Gifts of silver, wine and oil for the pharaoh

These two men in long robes are called viziers. They are the pharaoh's most important advisors.

Like everyone else who meets the pharaoh, these visitors from Syria are bowing very low.

What did he wear?

Flowing robes and amazing jewels. He had several different crowns. Most days, he wore a gold headband with a vulture and a snake made out of jewels. On special occasions, he wore a double crown, which was two crowns in one.

Vulture and snake Crown

Double Crown

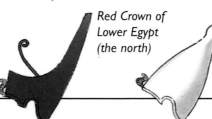

Red Crown of Lower Egypt (the north)

White Crown of Upper Egypt (the south)

Did he sit on the throne all day?

No, he was far too busy. He was in charge of the government, law, trade, and foreign policy. He was also the chief priest and army commander.

Here the pharaoh is inspecting sculptors building a new statue.

Paintings on the walls show scenes of life in Egypt.

One of these soldiers has just spotted a mouse.

Pillar decorated with hieroglyphs (Egyptian writing)

Visitors from Nubia (a land south of Egypt) with gifts of gold and ostrich eggs

This baboon doesn't want to meet the pharaoh.

Did the pharaohs have many wives?

Yes, but only one queen. She was usually the eldest daughter of the last king and queen.

Doesn't that mean he married his sister?

Yes, or his half-sister. This didn't seem odd to the Egyptians. Some of their gods were married to their brothers or sisters, too. Since the pharaoh was descended from the sun god, it was natural for him to do what the gods did.

Could a woman become pharaoh?

Not normally. If a very young boy became pharaoh, his mother could rule on his behalf. A few queens did act as kings. The most famous was a queen named Hatshepsut, who ruled successfully for many years.

Hatshepsut riding in her war chariot

11

Where did the Egyptians live?

In villages and towns on the banks of the Nile. Very few Egyptians lived anywhere else.

Why not?

Because the rest of Egypt was just a huge, hot desert. The Nile gave people water to drink and wash in. Deep floods made the land fertile and good for farming.

Didn't people's houses get flooded too?

Not unless the house was too close to the river. Most were built on higher ground, away from the banks. But, if the flood was much bigger than usual, animals, people and villages could be swept away.

Village

This man is suffering from the heat.

Fishing boats

Flint-bladed tools called sickles

This man is cooling down with a refreshing drink.

This house has been badly damaged in a flood.

The children are collecting the grain the men have missed.

Lunch arrving

This pole with a bucket is called a shaduf. It raises water into the fields.

This flute player is entertaining the harvesters.

This dog has run off with some of the picnic.

How often did the Nile flood?

Every spring, when rain and melted snow flowed into the river from the mountains in Ethiopia, south of Egypt. It made it so full that it overflowed and flooded the land. After a few weeks, the water level sank, leaving behind rich, fertile soil.

What did they grow?

All sorts of things. Melons, pomegranates, grapes, dates, figs, beans, peas, onions, garlic, leeks, lettuces and cucumbers. The main crops were wheat and barley for making bread and beer. They also grew flax, used for making linen clothes.

Did the farmers have tractors?

No, but they had strong oxen for pulling blades to break up the soil, and donkeys for carrying grain.

Did they keep animals?

Yes, all kinds. Cows, sheep, donkeys, goats, pigs, geese, ducks, pigeons, dogs and cats.

The best fields are closest to the river.

Can you spot the monkey? He looks as though he's stealing the dates. In fact, he's been specially trained to pick them.

The farmers have dug ditches and canals between the fields, to store floodwater and water the crops.

Granary for storing grain

This man has had a little too much beer with his lunch.

A difficult donkey

The cows are being made to stamp on the grain to separate it from the husks. This is called threshing.

These people are winnowing – tossing the grain in the air to separate it from the husk (the hard outside bit).

What did they do after the harvest?

Get ready for the next one. For a start, the ditches that carried water to the fields had to be mended. Then, many farmers were sent off to work on one of the pharaoh's building projects – perhaps to build a pyramid, a temple or a palace.

13

What were their houses like?

That depended on how rich the owners were. All Egyptian houses were made of mud brick, with wooden roofs covered with plaster and palm branches. Most had just one or two rooms, but rich people had cool, spacious villas, brightly painted inside, with gardens and pools.

The servants live here.

Grapevines

Wine press

Grain stores

Bedrooms

Reception hall

This enormous villa belongs to an extremely important man. You can find him in the reception hall receiving visitors.

The gatekeeper lives here. He keeps out unwelcome visitors.

These monkeys are helping the men to pick the dates. Of course they eat quite a few themselves.

This girl is taking an offering to the gods in the shrine (a small private temple).

How did they keep the houses cool?

Any way they could. Most houses had very thick walls and only very small, high windows. This helped to keep the sun out. Some houses had air vents on the roof too.

What was their furniture like?

Scarce. Even rich people didn't have much. Most people sat on stools (chairs were very special), and used chests to store things.

Simple wooden table

Chair made of ebony (an expensive dark wood) decorated with gold and ivory

Painted wooden chest

14

There is a stable for horses at the back.

In the kitchen, they're busy making lunch.

Central hall. They're having a party here on page 19.

Noisy geese

Brightly painted pillars

The roof is a good place to relax.

Cattle pens

Well for water

Simple pottery lamp

This magnificent stone lamp belongs to a pharaoh.

This pool is not for swimming. It's meant for keeping fish.

Musicians playing

How did they light their houses?

With lamps, made of clay or stone, which burned linseed oil. These lamps only gave off a very dim light though. They would have needed an awful lot of lamps to light their houses as brightly as ours.

Did they have bathrooms?

Yes they did, and toilets too. Keeping clean was very important to the Egyptians. Even the poorest people washed regularly in the Nile. In an expensive villa like this one, there was a stone-lined room where a servant poured water all over you. This was the nearest people got to having a shower.

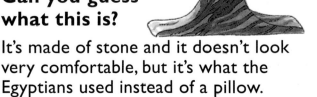

Can you guess what this is?

It's made of stone and it doesn't look very comfortable, but it's what the Egyptians used instead of a pillow. Apparently they slept quite well on them.

Did they care about fashion?

Most people were too hot to bother — but rich people spent a lot of time and money on looking good. Unlike today, though, their fashions changed quite slowly over about a thousand years.

These are the sort of clothes people wore in the Old and Middle Kingdoms.

Fancy kilt

Linen dress with shoulder straps

Hair padded with ornaments for a special occasion

A long kilt like this one means this man is old or quite important.

Sandals

Men wore kilts like these, made from cloth wrapped around and tied at the waist.

The barber has left a long braid of hair on this boy's head.

This wealthy woman is wearing a linen dress with an overdress of bright beads.

How did the styles change?

The dresses and kilts became looser and more flowing. Hairstyles were longer too, with a lot of braids and curls.

Children and adults often shaved their heads to keep them cool.

These are the sort of clothes people wore in the New Kingdom.

Underneath his wig, this man is probably bald.

Flowing cloak

Flowing, pleated dress, gathered with a belt

Tunic over kilt

What were the clothes made of?

Linen, from a plant called flax. The flax was spun into thread, then woven into cloth on a loom. Most linen cloth was probably plain white and undyed, though some people did wear bright

16 or patterned clothes.

Where did they wash them?

In the Nile, of course! They beat the clothes on stones to get rid of the dirt. There were no irons, so clothes were probably left to dry flat in the sun.

These women are weaving on an early loom. Later ones were upright.

Did they wear jewels?

Yes, absolutely everyone did. Men and women, rich and poor. They were made of many different materials; gold, silver, pottery, faience (a sort of glazed pottery) and semi-precious stones, such as turquoise and lapis lazuli.

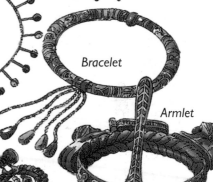

Beaded collar

Rings

Crown

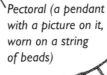

Pectoral (a pendant with a picture on it, worn on a string of beads)

Bracelet

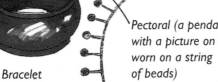

Bracelet

Armlet

Earrings

Did they wear perfume?

Yes, lots of it, made from flowers and scented wood soaked in oil. They also rubbed perfumed oil all over their bodies, to stop their skin from drying out.

Mirror made from polished metal

Chest for keeping cosmetics in

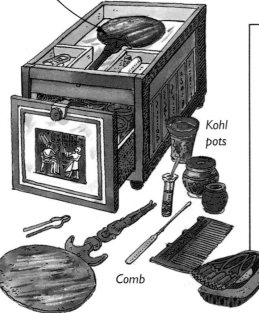

Kohl pots

Comb

Did they paint their faces?

Yes, both men and women outlined their eyes with dark green or grey paint called kohl. This was not just to look pretty – it helped keep away flies too! They also put red ochre (a kind of clay) on their cheeks and lips to make them redder. You could try to make yourself up like an Ancient Egyptian, using face paints.

17

What was Egyptian food like?

Very good. Their farms provided a wide variety of fruit and vegetables, meat, milk and cheese. People also caught fish in the river, and hunted wild animals and birds.

The people below are preparing food for the party on the page opposite.

Monkey enjoying juicy pomegranates

This boy is about to get an eyeful of fruit juice.

What food did they like best?

Sweet things, probably, such as cakes, pastries and fruits, washed down with barley beer or fruit wine. They had many different types of beer, of different quality and with different tastes.

Where did they do their cooking?

Usually outside. It was too dangerous to cook indoors. They used sticks, dried grass and animal dung as fuel.

One of the goats is having salad for lunch.

This party is taking place in the villa you saw on pages 14-15. There are a lot of foreign guests.

This guest has had a little too much pomegranate wine.

Lotus blossoms make the room smell nice

A rats' nest

Fan to keep the fire burning

Chargrilled fish

Spit-roasted goose

Rolling out the dough

A goose with a temper

Mud brick oven

The loaves will drop off when they are ready.

This dog loves freshly baked bread.

How did they keep things cool?

They didn't. The weather was pretty hot all year round and there were no refrigerators. So they had to eat everything quickly before it went bad.

How do we know what they ate?

Because some of the food has been found in graves. It looks very dried up now, after 3,000 years or more, but archeologists can still tell what it is. Wall paintings of temple offerings and parties also tell us what the food looked like.

More food from the kitchens

This dog loves stuffed goose.

This boy is going to bed. He's too young to stay up for the party.

All the food is being eaten with the fingers.

Can you spot the harp player?

The host and hostess are sitting on the raised platform.

Dancers

Lyre player

Flute player

A guest from Nubia

A well-fed pet

Jars of pomegranate wine

This guest has come from Syria with some interesting gossip.

These monkeys are trying to play with this pet goose. The goose looks a little annoyed.

What were their parties like?

Well, they look wonderful. Huge dishes of delicious food and wine, musicians, jugglers and dancers, and expensively dressed people in their best clothes and jewels.

Did you know?

Servants put cones of perfumed fat on the guests' heads. The fat melted and ran down their faces. It might sound disgusting, but it was probably very refreshing. How many cones can you spot in the main picture?

19

How did the Egyptians get around?

By boat, of course! The Nile was like a great highway, stretching up and down the country, with all sorts of different traffic. In any case, there were no roads.

Why not?

It was pointless to try to build roads in Egypt. They would have been covered and washed away by the floods every year.

This barge is carrying a huge stone statue called an obelisk. It\s going to be put outside a new temple further down the river. You can see it in position on page 27.

What kinds of boats did they have?

Fishing boats, funeral barges, luxurious boats for the royal family, cargo ships for transporting things such as stone blocks for the pyramids, and passenger ferries (which were usually overloaded). Can you spot the man who has fallen out?

The wind in Egypt usually blows from the north. This means the boats with their sails up are going south. For the boats going north, there is no wind to help them. They are the ones rowing.

Sea-going trading ship

The big boat below and to the right belongs to a rich nobleman.

These fishermen are dragging a net between their boats to catch the fish.

These boats are made of papyrus, a type of reed.

Did you know?

These are the Egyptian hieroglyphs for "south" (or "upstream") and "north (or "downstream"). Can you guess what they show? (Answers on page 32.)

This means "south".

This means "north".

How far did they sail?

Traders sailed to ports in the Eastern Mediterranean and the Red Sea. Some even went as far as Punt, a land in East Africa. They went looking for valuable myrrh trees, which gave them incense.

How did they travel on land?

Most Egyptians walked. The very rich were carried on special chairs. Merchants used donkeys for carrying things.

An Egyptian expedition to Punt

Myrrh tree

Didn't they have horses?

Not for the first 1,500 years. Even then, they were too expensive for most people.

Funeral barge

Carrying chair

Donkeys

Cargo boat

21

What did the Egyptians do for fun?

All sorts of things. They had no televisions or theatres, but they enjoyed watching royal processions and religious festivals. A popular way to relax was to spend a day hunting, fishing and picnicking on the river. For Egyptians, this was a little like going to the beach.

A tug-of-war shown on an Egyptian wall painting

What kinds of sports did they play?

As well as hunting and fishing, they enjoyed wrestling, fencing and energetic games like tug-of-war.

There are two men on the right hunting hippos. This is so dangerous, it usually takes a team of hunters to harpoon just one of them and bring it ashore with ropes and nets. These two must be very brave, and a bit mad, to try it alone.

Did they have any indoor games?

They had several types of board games, such as the two shown here, but nobody knows how they were played. They also loved singing, dancing and telling stories.

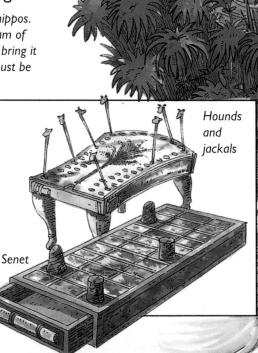

Monkeys eating dates

Hounds and jackals

Senet

Trying to tip over other boats is a popular sport.

A swim in the Nile is a good way of cooling off.

Papyrus reeds

Some people bring their pet cats hunting. The cats help to flush the birds out of the reeds.

The boats are made of papyrus reeds.

Luckily, this cat enjoys swimming.

What sort of toys did the children have?

Balls, spinning tops, dolls and wooden animals on wheels. Some toys even had moving parts – including a row of dancing dwarfs and a dog whose mouth opened.

A handle opens the dog's mouth.

Hippo made of painted pottery

Balls made of reeds and linen

Did they play music?

Yes, but there were no radios or MP3 players, so all music was live. We know the words of some of their songs, but we have no idea what the tunes were like.

What types of instruments did they have?

Plenty of different ones. They had wind instruments, such as pipes and flutes, and stringed instruments, such as lutes, harps and lyres. There were also drums, cymbals, tambourines and castanets.

Lute

Castanets

Harp

23

Did the Egyptians believe in God?

Not one God, but dozens of gods and goddesses. The Egyptians were a very religious people. They carved and built thousands of statues and temples, and painted pictures of the gods all over them.

What were their gods like?

Very different from each other. Some were quiet and gentle, others were fierce and terrifying. Each one was linked with a special animal or bird. To make them easy to recognize, the Egyptians often painted them with the head of that animal or bird.

Who were the most important ones?

It's hard to say. Isis, Osiris and Re (one version of the sun god) were among the most important. People believed Isis and Osiris had once been the King and Queen of Egypt.

Thoth, god of wisdom and writing, had the head of an ibis (a kind of bird).

Amun, King of the gods in the New Kingdom

Anubis, god of embalming. He had a jackal's head.

Tawaret, a female hippopotamus, looked after pregnant women and babies.

Osiris, son of Geb and Nut, ruler of the dead

Bast, a mother goddess. She is shown as a cat.

Horus, god of the sky, son of Isis and Osiris

This version of Re, the sun god, shows him with a falcon's head.

Isis, goddess of crafts, sister and wife of Osiris

Geb, god of the Earth

Ma'at, goddess of truth and justice

Who was the most popular god?

Probably Bes the dwarf, because he was so funny. He made the other gods laugh, and looked after people's homes and children.

Were there any stories about them?

Yes, hundreds. Many gods and goddesses were related and married to each other. Their lives were full of feuds and fights and other adventures. You can read one of these stories on the next page...

There are many legends about Re,
the mighty sun god
and creator of the universe.
This one tells of how he nearly caused
the death of humankind,
and how he finally saved it.

The lioness and the red river

From the beginning, people had a great respect for Re. They feared him, for he was the most powerful god of all. Yet, as the years passed, there were those who thought Re must be growing old – and surely an old god must be weak and feeble?

Some people stopped their worship of Re altogether. Worse still, there were others who plotted his downfall. When this news reached the sun god, he flew into a violent rage. He orderd Hathor, the goddess of beauty, to go down to Earth immediately. Her mission was to destroy every single person who had plotted against him or insulted him.

Hathor went to Earth in the form of a lioness, with mighty paws, powerful jaws and terrifying teeth. She started by killing Re's enemies as instructed, but soon found she so loved the taste of human blood that she started hunting down and killing everyone. Even Re's most faithful followers were not safe from Hathor's thirst for blood.

When Re saw what was happening, he knew that he must act quickly to stop what he had started. While Hathor slept, he flooded Egypt with a very strong, red beer. When the gooddess awoke, she saw the red beer and thought it was human blood. Full of excitement, she began to lap it up. Mixed with strong magic, the beer made Hathor very happy. Soon she was so happy that she forgot her mission, and her taste for human blood. She returned home with a headache, but then she changed back to her usual loving self.

On very rare occasions, the water in the Nile is a rusty red.
Perhaps this is a reminder from Re that he may be old
but is still all-powerful. Or perhaps it is because
the water carries red dust blown by the wind
from the Sahara Desert.
Who knows?

Where did they worship their gods and goddesses?

Some family gods, like Bes and Tawaret, were worshipped at home. The more important ones had their own temples.

What went on in a temple?

Priests and priestesses conducted special services in front of a statue. The Egyptians believed the god's spirit entered the statue to receive offerings and prayers. Sometimes the pharaoh and queen were there, but nobody else.

Didn't ordinary people go inside?

No. They had to pray outside. People were only allowed in on very special occasions, such as after the birth of a child. They saw the statue on festival days, though. Then it was carried through the streets on a golden painted boat.

This is the festival of Bast, the cat goddess. She is very popular with everyone.

The statues in rows are called sphinxes. They have the bodies of lions and the heads of rams.

These tall, pointy things are called obelisks. They are monuments to the sun god.

The priests and priestesses are leading the way.

These cows are going to be sacrificed.

Flute-playing priestesses

Statue of Bast

How many temples were there?

Probably thousands. Even today, you can see the ruins of hundreds of them all along the banks of the Nile.

Priests

Breakfast

Priestesses singing and dancing

The god lives in here

What happened at a service?

First thing in the morning, the priests woke the god, washed the statue, covered it with perfume, dressed it and gave it food. There were prayers, music and dancing too. In the evening, the statue was put to bed.

This is a New Kingdom temple. There are many outbuildings inside the temple walls – a library, a school, craft workshops and a house for the priests.

The walls are carved and painted all over with pictures and picture writing. You can find out more about the writing on pages 30-31.

This dog is terrified of cats — especially cat goddesses.

These boys are hoping for a closer look.

Did you know?

Some people used to put a carving like this, of a pair of ears, outside the temple walls. They hoped it would remind the god to listen to their prayers.

Did they believe in heaven?

Yes, but they called it the "Fields of the Blessed". All dead people were judged by the god Osiris. If they had led good lives, they lived happily ever after. For bad people, there was an evil, hungry monster waiting to gobble them up.

What were their towns and cities like?

Hot, dusty, noisy and crowded. They were very dirty too, as people threw all their garbage out into the street.

Didn't that make them very smelly places?

Surprisingly not. The heat was so strong that things dried up very quickly, and this stopped them from smelling too much.

Did they use money?

Not until a thousand years after pyramid times. Until then, people just exchanged things that were worth about the same. There could be problems though, if they disagreed about the price.

It's market day at this busy Egyptian town.

Fetching water

Did they have skyscrapers?

Not like modern ones. But building land was so valuable that many townhouses were very narrow and tall, sometimes as much as three or four floors high.

Unloading cargo

Where did people do their shopping?

At market stalls in the street. They sold everything from locally grown fruit and vegetables to cloth, furniture and exotic goods from other countries. There were refreshment stalls too, selling beer to thirsty shoppers. This was much thicker than modern beer, a little like soup, and very strong.

28

Was there much crime?

Egyptian towns and cities had their share of shady characters – robbers, murderers and people who tried to sell stolen goods.

Can you spot a man ducking to avoid being splashed?

Did they have prisons?

No. But criminals were often locked up in temples before a trial. (The walls were too high to escape easily). Punishment included flogging, exile (being sent away) and death.

Temple

Cooking breakfast

This is the donkey that was causing trouble on page 13.

Did they have a police force?

Yes. They were called the Medjay. Their job was to keep law and order and catch criminals. In the country, they used dogs to help them track down suspects. Can you spot one here, chasing a thief?

Could the Egyptians read and write?

Yes. They were among the first to invent it, but very few people knew how. People called scribes had the job of reading and writing for everyone else.

What did their writing look like?

Like pictures or signs. We call them hieroglyphs and there are over 700 of them. There are hieroglyphs for a single letter, some for a group of letters, and others for a whole word.

The Egyptians didn't have an alphabet like ours, and their language didn't have exactly the same sounds as ours. The alphabet on the right is the closest we can get to matching our modern-day letters.

An A to Z of hieroglyphs

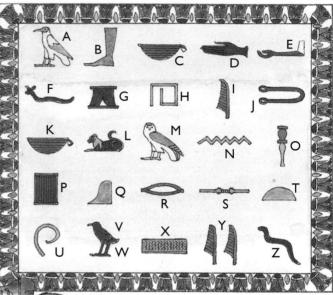

Hieroglyphs can be written from left to right, or right to left, or in columns, as they are in this wall painting.

Always start reading from the direction the animal or people signs are facing. This means you read the alphabet above from left to right, as we do.

Egyptian painting follows special rules. People look as if they are painted from several angles at once.

The eyes look straight ahead.

The shoulders are drawn from the front.

People's faces, legs and chest are always shown from the side.

What did they write on?

Special paper, called papyrus (made from reeds) or bits of broken pottery. They used wooden brushes or pens to write with. They also carved words all over the walls of temples and other buildings.

Pens

Papyrus

Inks

Why did they do that?

Because they believed writing had special magic powers. Hieroglyph means "holy writing" in Greek. The Egyptian name for it was "words of the gods".

Did Egyptian children go to school?

A few boys did, but usually only the rich ones. Most children worked in the fields when they were old enough, or learned a trade or a craft. Girls usually helped their mothers, and girls from richer families might learn to read and write at home.

Boys at a temple school

They are using bits of broken pottery to write on. Papyrus is too expensive.

The teachers are scribes.

What different jobs were there?

Many Egyptians were farmers, but there were many different craftsmen and women too. A boy could also become a soldier. The best job was to be a scribe, a priest, a court official or a doctor. Egyptian doctors were so skilled that they were even famous in other countries.

Paper-maker

Maid

Leatherworker

Carpenter

Mourner

Stone vase maker

Musician

Scribe

Priestess

Weaver

Perfume maker

Dancer

Doctor

Potter

Soldier

Sculptor

Write your name in hieroglyphs

You could write your own name, using the hieroglyphs on page 30. Pharaohs' names were written inside an oval shape, like this, called a cartouche. Egyptian words were spelled in a complicated way, so you won't recognize all the hieroglyphs. You should be able to figure out one of them though.

This is the cartouche of the pharaoh Meryre.

Index

Answers
Page 19
There are eight cones.
Page 20
One boat under sail, and
one with its sail down.

This edition first published in 2015 by Usborne
Publishing Ltd, 83-35 Saffron Hill, London
EC1N 8RT, England. www.usborne.com

Copyright © 2015, 1995 Usborne Publishing Ltd.
The name Usborne and the devices 🔱 🎈
are Trade Marks of Usborne Publishing Ltd.

All rights reserved. No part of this publication
may be reproduced, stored in a retrieval system
or transmitted in any form or by any means,
electronic, mechanical, photocopying, recording
or otherwise, without the prior permission of
the publisher. UKE